IMAGES OF ENGLAND

Mitcham

For Ann

IMAGES OF ENGLAND

Mitcham

Nick Harris

NONSUCH

First published 1996
This new pocket edition 2006
Images unchanged from first edition

Nonsuch Publishing Limited
The Mill, Brimscombe Port,
Stroud, Gloucestershire, GL5 2QG
www.nonsuch-publishing.com

Nonsuch Publishing is an imprint of Tempus Publishing Group

British Library Cataloguing in Publication Data.
A catalogue record for this book is available from the British Library.

ISBN 1-84588-298-9

Typesetting and origination by Nonsuch Publishing Limited
Printed in Great Britain by Oaklands Book Services Limited

Contents

Acknowledgements

With thanks to Heather Morton, Susan Andrew and all the Mitcham library staff, their excellent collection at London Road is well worth further investigation.

This book would not have been possible without the help of all those individuals who have donated their photographs to the library. These include:

Mrs M. Gutteridge, F. Wells, Mr F.P. Olney, Mr E.G. Clothier, Mr A.E. Gibson, J. MacGuiness, Sydney W. Mewbury, Mr G.W. Rowbotham and Miss P. Crawford.

I am sure others have performed the same service and apologise for any omissions. The library is always happy to provide a good home for prints of, or your collection of, local interest photographs.

Efforts to trace the copyright holder for the photographs taken by Mr Marcus, Clifford Fox, the *Mitcham News* (and *Mercury*) and the *Mitcham and Tooting Advertiser*, proved fruitless but I am grateful to them all.

A final acknowledgement to all those who helped with the preparation of the text – they know who they are!

Introduction

Only in recent years have the efforts of local historians, particularly those of Eric Montague (in *Mitcham, A Pictorial History* and *Tom Francis' Mitcham*), gone some way to providing Mitcham with the recognition which its fascinating past deserves. This book concentrates on the social history, particularly in the twentieth century, of a town which is too often portrayed as characterless and without roots. This could not be further from the truth.

While archaeological evidence suggests Prehistoric and Roman activity, written evidence exists from Saxon times of a permanent settlement. The Domesday Book, a nationwide census commissioned by William the Conqueror in 1086, records 250 people living in 2 hamlets – Mitcham (modern Upper Mitcham) and Whitford (the area around and to the south of Lower Green). The four manors which comprised Mitcham in the Middle Ages remained sparsely populated but the parish became highly fashionable in the reign of Elizabeth I. Both the explorer, Walter Raleigh, and poet, John Donne, resided here for a time and the Monarch herself stayed in the area on five occasions.

By the time of the Civil War, in 1642, Mitcham had become a prosperous agricultural village and a magnet for wealthy merchants and those seeking refuge from the rigours of London life. Prominent among these was Robert Cranmer. He had purchased the manor of Mitcham Canons by 1653 and his family remained landlords for five generations. The Canons and other fine houses, some of which still stand, are the legacy of increasing trade in the Stuart and Georgian periods which saw wealth flood into Mitcham. The village became known as the 'Montpelier of England' due to its fine air which was a blessing for Londoners escaping the plague – the worst outbreak of which decimated the city's population in 1665. Mitcham also became an important halting post on the route from London to Brighton and inns such as the King's Head, which survives today as the Burn Bullock, sprung up along the route. Milestones at Figges Marsh and Lower Green West still testify to a time when tollgates exacted taxes from road users at Colliers Wood and Figges Marsh.

The eighteenth and nineteenth centuries were marked by the ascendancy of industry – cultivation and distillation of essential oils such as peppermint and lavender at the works of Ephraim Potter and William Moore and the processing of textiles, snuff, flour and paper along the Wandle. The Surrey Iron Railway, opened in 1803, which stopped at Mitcham en route from Wandsworth to Croydon, was the first public railway in the world.

Its collapse in the 1830s with the advent of steam locomotives was a watershed in Mitcham's fortunes. The town was skirted by the new railway system and thus did not enjoy the suburban expansion of neighbouring Wimbledon and Croydon. The arrival of such anti-social industries as paint, varnish and linoleum manufacture coincided with the exodus of the wealthy families. It was the death knell for major horticultural enterprise in the area (Potter and Moore broke up in 1886) and Mitcham's rural atmosphere disappeared as the population doubled to 29,606 between 1900 and 1910.

The archaic administrative structure could not cope with this expansion and Mitcham was run by a succession of bodies before its incorporation into the new London Borough of Merton in 1965, completing the transition from a semi-feudal to a municipal society in less than a century. The main objective of the new authorities was to erect housing, especially in the years following the First World War – 'Homes for Heroes' was the rallying cry. Much of Mitcham was developed by 1930 but the permanence of today's open spaces was also enshrined. The achievement of borough status in 1934 was built on the expansion of local industry and Mitcham's position as a booming dormitory town. Inter-war development was surpassed by the post Second World War housing schemes which set in motion the huge changes to the area which are well within living memory.

Many have seen this transition as a move for the worse, the eight-year absence of the fair a sign of the loss of village solidarity. However if the return of the fair in 1983 leads to a resurrection of the civic responsibility which has served Mitcham so well in the past, the future will be bright.

One

The Lower Greens
and Church Road

The Vestry Hall, decorated for the Diamond Jubilee of Queen Victoria, December 1897. After a thirty-year period as Mitcham Town Hall, the building reverted to its original name in 1965. The building on the left is the old Cricketers pub, which was destroyed by a bomb in 1940 (see page 107). The photograph is one of a collection of pictorial records of Mitcham made by a committee who were nominated by the Parish Council in 1901.

The Cricket Green, c.1910. The Vestry Hall can be seen in the left hand corner. The old Methodist church is on the far right hand side in the position which is now occupied by its replacement.

The Cricket Green, c. 1911. Notice the fashions of the day, including the ubiquitous summer hat. The building on the left remains as two private cottages.

One of a series of postcards of Mitcham from the late 1940s, a view of London Road which is very familiar today. The bank has closed, the White Hart awaits refurbishment while the former hairdressers is vacant at present. A seventeenth-century indenture of sale referring to the pub still exists.

A cricket match in progress on the Cricket Green, c.1890. This view looks towards the corner of Whitford Lane (now London Road) and Lower Green West and X marks the site of Doctor Shelswell's house, which later became Sibford (see page 22).

Looking south across the Cricket Green at a more contemporary game, in the 1960s. The buildings in the background are unchanged from this view.

The Bedser twins open the new Cricketers pub, the replacement for its bomb-damaged predecessor (see page 10), in 1958. The twins, pictured beside the horses, were very famous Surrey cricketers of the time. The men in bowler-hats were draymen from Young & Co., the Wandsworth brewers.

Ye Olde King's Head, Mitcham.

J. J. Kenyon, Mitcham.

The Georgian front block of the King's Head pub. The timber-framed, tile-hung rear dates from the sixteenth or seventeenth century but the bow window, 'shell' porch (at the side) and heavy cornice are Edwardian additions. The Parish Council met here before the Vestry Hall was built and special hearings of the Magistrates' Court were held during Mitcham Fair. The name was changed to the Burn Bullock in 1975 to commemorate its well known, late, licensee and Surrey cricketer.

Old houses on the Causeway (the ancient name for the southern side of the Cricket Green), c.1910. The tall building with the chimneys on the middle right of the picture is the old police station which has provided the site for the force's modern building. The pub sign in the middle refers to the Brittania, another Youngs establishment, which can just be glimpsed on the right.

Construction of the present Methodist church, in 1959, on the site of its predecessor (see page 10). The view is from the grounds of the Canons.

A first communicants' procession from Saints Peter and Paul's Roman Catholic church, 1962. The procession has been an annual event around the Cricket Green since the beginning of the twentieth century.

The tiny original Catholic chapel which was built in 1861/2 on the south side of the Cricket Green, off the Causeway, near the almshouses. The site is now occupied by the Saints Peter and Paul Primary School.

Left: Felling of the last remaining elm tree on the Cricket Green in September 1973 after attempts to save them with inoculation fluid had failed. The almshouses, dating back to 1829, can be seen in the background.

Below: The great tithe barn which stood in the yard of Cranmer farm. Tithes, a medieval tax amounting to one tenth of farm produce, were paid to the Church until the Reformation. The right to the tithes was purchased by Robert Cranmer in 1656. The barn was pulled down in the 1920s to make way for the erection of the Wilson Hospital and the Mitcham County School for Girls (see pages 86 and 108).

Cold Blows, a footpath leading from the Cricket Green to Three Kings Piece. The name appears in documents dating from the seventeenth century.

Canons House in 1988. Built in 1680, it was one of the properties on the Cranmer estate. It was named after the Canons of St Mary Overy at Southwark, who had owned the land until the dissolution of the monasteries. It is now used as a meeting place and recreation centre and the basement houses a museum and heritage centre.

A view of the newly-completed present Catholic church and Cranmers, 1895. Another house on the estate, near the tithe barn (see page 16), it was also demolished for the erection of the Wilson Hospital, as were the old houses to the left of the picture. The White Hart can be seen in the extreme background.

ELIZABETHAN COTTAGE   4075

An Elizabethan cottage which had started to fall down by the time this photo was taken in 1930. The site, overlooking Lower Green West, housed a timber yard and is now occupied by Beadle Court, an aptly-named block of flats providing police accommodation.

Looking towards the church, along Church Road, c.1900. The grounds of Hall Place are on the left and the Bull pub can be made out in the middle of the picture. The wooden buildings have all disappeared, to be replaced by housing dating from differing times throughout this century.

The Bull at the junction of Church Road and Church Place, c.1900. The pub was recorded in the eighteenth century and is still run by Youngs. H.J. Chubb was a butchers shop but the building is now offices.

Looking along Church Path at Mitcham parish church, 1952. The gardens of the vicarage are over the wall to the right. This view is unchanged now except for the pinnacles on the church tower which were removed in 1956.

Looking east, toward the altar of the parish church, c.1870. The reading desk was dedicated to the memory of Collingwood Denny, the nephew of Lord Collingwood who took command at the Battle of Trafalgar after the death of Lord Nelson.

The former west entrance to the church, in 1870, showing the tomb of Sir Ambrose Crowley who died in 1713. The entrance has been closed off with a row of windows behind which stands the baptistry. One now enters the church through the porch on the south side.

Mrs Everett, the pew opener at the church, photographed in 1875. At this time, parishioners would pay a rent for a family pew and Mrs Everett would unlock it for them on their arrival at the church.

Left: Lady Lewisham, a former member of the Greater London Council, stepmother of Princess Diana and daughter of Dame Barbara Cartland with Mr (formerly Alderman) W. Jeffrey at the opening of Sibford, which had been converted into twelve flatlets for the elderly in 1958.

Below: Sibford, in 1958, at the corner of London Road and Lower Green West.

Two

Colliers Wood
and Phipps Bridge

Looking south along the High Street, Colliers Wood in 1952. In the far distance on the left hand side is Colliers Wood underground station. This view is little changed now.

Further along the High Street in 1958. These weatherboard and pantile cottages were a very common eighteenth-century construction in Surrey. They were pulled down soon after this picture was taken and provided the site for the Colliers Wood Community Centre.

Looking north along Colliers Wood High Street, c.1920. The cottages in the previous picture are visible on the near left hand side and the Red Lion pub is in the middle on the left. The adjacent terrace of shops still remains.

Further south along the High Street, after the introduction of the tramway in 1906.

Above: The Singlegate turnpike, situated at what is now the junction of the High Street and Christchurch Road, *c.*1865. Tolls were abolished in 1870 and the tube station now stands on the site of this eighteenth-century building.

Left: Floods from the overflowing Wandle at Singlegate, *c.*1885. The turnpike gave its name to the area and its primary school.

The *South Londoner* waits at Platform One of Merton Abbey station in 1958. Opened in 1868, the station was closed to regular passenger traffic in 1929. The buildings of Tandem Works, demolished in 1995, can be seen in the left background. All traces of this line, which ran across the site of Merton Priory, have now disappeared. The site was excavated by the Museum of London and the remains of the Chapter House of the Priory which lay underneath the station have been preserved under Merantun Way.

Pupils at Singlegate School at the turn of the twentieth century. The school house survives at the junction of Christchurch Road and Prince George's Road but no longer serves the same purpose.

Outside the Albion, which was demolished for the widening of Church Road and Phipps Bridge Road, now called Liberty Avenue. The remainder of the site was used for new housing.

The Keeper's Lodge, a gothic building in the grounds of Wandle Villa, on Phipps Bridge Road, which is now National Trust property. The house on the right is believed to have been the residence of Edward Asprey, a member of the family who founded the world-famous shop in Bond Street, in the 1840s.

An old house on the corner of Liberty Avenue (then Phipps Bridge Road) in 1912. This site was also largely absorbed in road widening.

Left: The demolition of two blocks of the former Holborn Union Workhouse then the James Factory Estate, in Western Road, *c.*1960. The workhouse was built by the Guardians of the Poor of the Holborn Union in 1886. After the reform of the Poor Law, in 1929, the buildings became redundant and were let out as factory units. The site has now been redeveloped for various commercial purposes.

Below: Old houses in Half-Acre Row, *c.*1875. Half-Acre Row was a turning to the south of Western Road between the Gladstone off-licence and the gas works. The houses were bought by George Pitt, a prominent Quaker shopkeeper, re-conditioned and re-named by him, 'Resurrection Place'. The site is now a vacant lot on Fieldgate Lane.

Aerial view of Phipps Bridge, 10 February, 1954. In the right foreground is the council's Homeward Road refuse destructor and in the centre of the picture are prefabricated bungalows and the Rock Terrace recreation ground. This was all cleared away in the early '60s for the Phipps Bridge housing estate. The Wimbledon to Croydon railway is on the left and in the distance is Bunce's Meadow and the Wandle.

Looking along Bath Road, which can be seen in the previous photo in front of the prefabs, towards New Close housing estate in Phipps Bridge Road. This view is from 1959, just before the clearance for the new estate began.

The Western Road gas works, 1870, adjacent to Half-Acre Row (see page 30). This building has gone but the site, owned by British Gas, remains involved with gas distribution and a gas holder still stands. Until the 1950s, it was a gas making site - coal was clamped down in vertical retorts and then heated to drive off the gas and tar. Charging the retorts and their opening to discharge the incandescent coke gave rise to clouds of yellow smoke, which gave the area a distinctive and unpleasant aroma.

Mitcham and Wimbledon Gas Company brass band, c.1908. The two separate companies amalgamated at the beginning of the century. Many people spent their entire working lives with the company, of which they were extremely proud and this feeling was reflected in the band which had an excellent reputation throughout the south east.

WANDSWORTH, WIMBLEDON &
EPSOM GAS Cº
VIEWS OF MITCHAM WORKS

A further amalgamation led to the formation of this company by the 1930s.

A more familiar view after the gas making department of the works closed on 1 May, 1960 following ninety-three years of production. The house in front of the gas holder was built in 1851 and used as the company's offices but has since disappeared.

Dr Love and Mrs Wray at the Woodlands Maternity and Child Welfare Centre, in Colliers Wood, 1920.

Three

Around the Upper, or Fair, Green

Looking north at Fair Green in 1924. London Road and Fair Green are in the centre of the picture and the buildings of the Holborn Union Workhouse are in the top left-hand corner.

A similar view from the late 1940s. The main difference to the previous picture is the appearance of the Majestic cinema, the large building in the right foreground.

Upper Green West in 1935, looking towards Western Road. The building in the foreground is the eighteenth-century Nag's Head which was replaced by another pub with the same name but has since been demolished.

A similar view from 1962. In the centre is the Fair Green market which was cleared away during road works in the 1980s. Western Road is on the left and the Nag's Head is behind the trees on the right.

Loafers by the village pump on
Fair Green in 1890. The pump was
replaced by the Jubilee clock tower.
This north-facing view includes a row
of charming wooden buildings in
London Road, long since demolished.

The clock tower, erected to celebrate Queen
Victoria's Diamond Jubilee of 1897, in 1959.
The bollards in front of the tower can also be
seen in the previous picture.

Above: Upper Green East in 1953. The whole of this area was completely relandscaped in the early 1990s. The Kings Arms, which, in 1900, replaced the wooden cottages on the previous page, can be seen in the right background.

Right: The north side of Upper Green looking towards the junction of St Marks Road and London Road in 1934. The Majestic cinema was demolished in the 1970s to make way for a supermarket.

St Mark's church, which dates from 1905, photographed in 1959.

Upper Green East or Fair Green, looking towards the Majestic cinema in 1955. Apart from the redirection of the traffic, landscaping and demolition of the cinema, this view remains similar today.

A view from Fair Green towards the Common and Croydon between 1906, when the tram service began, and the outbreak of the First World War.

A close-up of Woods' confectioners and Ruff's boot and shoe shop at Fair Green, c.1910. The businesses have changed but the buildings and old world atmosphere remain.

The gardens at Upper Green East in 1957. The eighteenth-century building in the middle, P. Gutteridge and Son's corn and forage shop, was demolished in the 1970s and replaced by the present red-brick building of Barclay's bank.

Looking south from the upper windows of the cinema down London Road towards the Cricket Green in 1961. The Common lies to the left and Western Road is away to the right.

Above: Looking north from further down London Road in the 1950s. The telephone exchange is on the right but at this time it also included a post office, since relocated to the Upper Green.

Right: London Road, immediately to the south of Fair Green, *c.*1910. London House, a large general store owned by the Francis family, can just be seen on the left. The store and the two adjoining houses were demolished in the 1950s for the present row of shops and offices.

Huge crowds were drawn to the opening ceremony of the Mitcham Fair on 12 August, 1935. The Fair was held on Three Kings Piece, whence it had been moved when the original site at Fair Green could no longer accommodate the throng in the 1920s.

The formal opening of the Fair in 1932. As today, the key played an important symbolic role in the ceremony, and would be held aloft by the Chairman of the Urban District Council or, after 1934, the Mayor of the Borough.

Four

Upper Mitcham
and North Mitcham

High Street (which became the London Road in 1936), Upper Mitcham, looking towards Collbran's Corner and the Fair Green, c.1900. Collbran's Corner is on the west of the junction of the road from London and Upper Green. The King's Arms can be seen in the distance on the right and the Buck's Head is on the left.

Looking south from further along the London Road in 1959. The road was pedestrianised in 1994 and the fisheries shop has become a second hand furniture outlet.

London Road Boy's School in 1925. Both this building (which dates from 1855) and Eagle House to its right are still standing.

The early-eighteenth-century Eagle House which is Grade II listed. It has been refurbished recently and is now occupied by offices.

The Holborn Schools building, with accommodation for 400 boys, girls and infants, was part of the extensive Holborn Union workhouse complex. London unions often sought cheaper land in the countryside to provide workhouses for their poor and orphans. It was built in 1856 in London Road to the north of Eagle House where Monarch Parade is today. The pond in the foreground was one of many in Mitcham and was filled in with spoil from the excavation of the Northern Line. The market garden firm of Mizen Brothers erected greenhouses here on what had been Pound Farm. These were later demolished after being severely damaged in the Second World War and Armfield Crescent was built on the site.

A 'crocodile' of Union School children in London Road, 1913.

The 'Elms', a children's home, after a catastrophic fire on Christmas Eve, 1891. Formerly the residence of Peter Waldo, it passed into the hands of his successors, the Waldo Sibthorp family. Standing on the east side of London Road it provided the site for the shops erected in 1934, immediately north of the public baths.

The baths in 1932. This site is now crossed by a road leading to the multi-storey car park.

Looking north along London Road in 1952. Eagle House is on the left, Monarch Parade (see page 48) is in the middle and the baths building is in the right foreground.

A view from the library window looking north along London Road near the Swan towards Figges Marsh in 1952.

Laburnum Road estate, off Eastfields Road, under construction in 1956.

The junction of London Road and Eveline Road, c.1929. The Swan pub can be seen on the far left. The buildings on either side of Eveline Road were erected on the site of Potter and Moore's lavender distillery.

Poplars Boarding School at Figges Marsh, named after the large poplar trees at its front which were all blown down soon after this photograph, c.1875, but before the house was demolished around 1880. The building stood on the west side of London Road on the site now occupied by Poplar Avenue.

Further north along London Road in 1952, approaching Tooting Junction station, with Figges Marsh on the right.

North Mitcham Bazaar, 18 November 1938. Helpers of the Mitcham Improvement Association tempt the Mayor, Alderman East, and Mayoress with their wares.

Looking south along Streatham Road towards Mitcham, September 1930. Caithness Road is on the left while Ashbourne Road runs off to the right. Apart from the influx of traffic, this view remains largely unchanged.

The new Edwardian housing in Caithness Road, off Streatham Road, c. 1910.

54

Slightly larger accommodation in St Barnabas Road, on the other side of Streatham Road, c. 1920.

The ornamental pond off the drive leading to Gorringe Park House, c. 1900. The drive has since become Gorringe Park Avenue.

Above: An aerial photograph in the early 1950s. Mitcham Stadium is in the foreground, the Royal Arsenal Co-operative Society's dairy and bakery is on the left and the nearby Pascall's sweet factory can be identified by its chimney. Streatham Road is in the top left hand corner and Edgehill Road runs parallel with the railway line on the right.

Left: Workers at James Pascall & Co., c.1950. After an amalgamation in 1959, the factory was demolished and the site has been redeveloped as an industrial estate.

Five

Eastfields, Pollards Hill
and the Common

Eastfields level crossing, looking north-east, in 1956. The ground is under cultivation by Mizens, market gardeners, who moved away to Woking. The site has since become the playing fields of Eastfields School. Pains fireworks factory can be seen in the distance. This has also disappeared, a housing estate standing in its place.

The level crossing is all that survived from the previous view into the 1960s. Further change was inevitable – the signal box and the old gates have both now disappeared.

Houses in Manor Way, soon after their completion in the 1920s. At this time estates were often developed before the road was made up. The local authority then had to 'adopt' the road and apportion charges on frontages for its surfacing and drainage. The unsatisfactory state of the unmade roads led to the emergence of vociferous residents' associations.

Road surfacing is underway in Avenue Road in 1929.

Left: Lenny Bruce undertakes vital duties at Liberty Cafe in Manor Road, 1974.

Below: An aerial view of Pollards Hill housing estate, 1956. An immense postwar development on the former Pollards Hill golf course, it comprised at first pre-fabricated bungalows and houses. The bungalows have all been replaced by permanent houses or blocks of flats, the first of which are under construction here.

Numbers 205 and 207 Commonside East, 1959. Built around 1853, No. 207 was extended in the 1930s while Alderman Dalton, a mayor of Mitcham, lived at No. 205.

A temporary stalemate at Mitcham Common during the unsuccessful protest against the tipping of household refuse by the borough council in June 1954.

Unemployed men occupied by public works on the Common, *c.*1900.

Seven Islands Pond, Mitcham Common, *c.*1930. Previously a gravel pit, it was deepened, marked off with posts and draped with old tyres to create Mitcham's first swimming pool.

Above: Haymaking on the Common in 1954. This area, near the Croydon boundary, has now been substantially relandscaped following tipping (see page 60).

Right: Laying two miles of gas pipe through Mitcham Common in 1958.

Gypsies on Mitcham Common, 1881. This photograph is part of a series taken by members of Croydon Camera Club which document the rich fabric of Mitcham life around the turn of the century and provide some of the most interesting material for this book.

The funeral of a Sophie Karpath, the daughter of the chief of the Galician gypsy tribe encamped at Beddington Corner on the edge of Mitcham Common in 1911. The coffin was borne to the parish church, where the lid was removed and the mourners advanced to take a final look at the deceased who was robed as for a festival in a scarlet frock and adorned in valuable jewellery. The verger at this time was a Mr Champion who, after the funeral, had a visit from the interpreter, complaining bitterly that he had not been paid for his services. He asked for the loan of a pick and shovel so that he could dig up the coffin and take his fee in the jewellery that adorned the corpse. The request was refused.

Beddington Lane Halt station in 1951 on the West Croydon to Wimbledon line.

Mr William Baker, station master of Mitcham Junction, shortly before his retirement in 1961.

'Remember the Grotto', *c.*1930. Children used to build pretty structures in an attempt to collect pennies from passers-by which they would spend at Mitcham Fair.

Removal of the tram lines in the main road through the Common in 1942, the trams having been replaced by trolleybuses. The pylons on the side of the road are set to carry the electric wires which powered the trolleybuses.

A trolleybus at the Ravensbury Arms stop on the Common in 1958.

The Ravensbury Arms, also known as the Blue House, c.1920. Built in 1906, this red-brick building replaced a weatherboarded predecessor. Cattle used to wander freely on the Common and the pound for strays was at the rear of the pub. The distance from the Blue House to the Red House (the Jolly Gardeners) is a mile and many pony and foot races were run between the two.

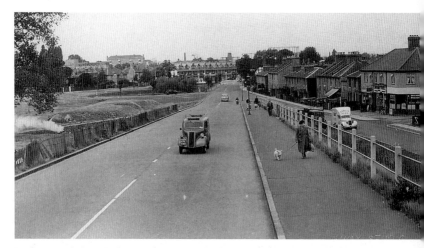

Looking north from Beehive Bridge, Commonside East in 1953. A view which is little changed today.

Smith's buildings from Commonside East. A row of back-to-back houses, they stood a few yards west of the Beehive pub and were demolished under a slum clearance order in 1936. This allowed room to widen the bridge over the railway. Sparrowhawk's scrap yard was close by, beside the bridge.

Above: A mobile Methodist preacher provokes a variety of reactions from his predominantly young audience on Three Kings Piece in 1958.

Right: Fishing for tiddlers in Three Kings Pond in the same year. A pastime which would now attract a £100 fine and provide very little reward.

The eighteenth-century Park Place, on Commonside West, in 1974. It was used between the wars as the clubhouse of the *News of the World* organisation.

The start of the annual, *News of the World*, London to Brighton relay race in 1938.

Six

Lower Mitcham

Looking south down London Road towards Mitcham station at the junction with the Cricket Green in 1959. The policeman seems to be walking towards the Kings Head for a mid-day pint! All the buildings except the inn, which is Grade II listed, have been replaced by office blocks.

London Road, a little further to the south, c.1930. C.E. Spence, newsagents and Stevenson & Rush, grocers, can be seen on the left. On the right is Allen Bros, motor mechanics, who still trade, but in new premises alongside the tyre and exhaust centre.

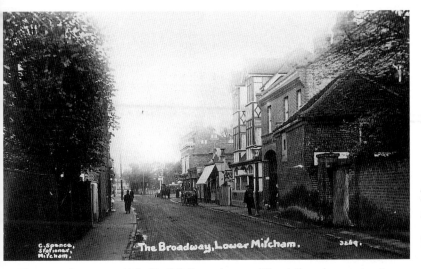

This postcard view was published by C.E. Spence (see page 72) and shows the same situation but looking north towards the Cricket Green in 1904. This section was known as the Broadway but was in fact one of the narrowest parts of London Road and has since been widened, necessitating the demolition of all the buildings in this photo.

Looking north along London Road in 1949. The land on the left is now occupied by blocks of flats.

A Stevenson & Rush delivery cart in 1900 (see page 72).

Mitcham Congregational church, which stood in London Road between the Cricket Green and Mitcham station, c.1935. It was demolished in 1993 and the site is now occupied by Temple Gate Mews, an estate of small houses.

An early photo of a foreman and his men outside Baron House, *c.*1870. Baron House has long been demolished and is now replaced by council flats, one block of which is called Baron Court.

Bishopsford Road and its bridge over the Wandle, c.1900. A new bridge has since been built which covers over the ford but the arches of the old bridge can still be seen.

The water wheel at the Mitcham hair and fibre mills on the Wandle in January 1959, five years before the mill was destroyed by fire.

76

The Crown Mill and nearby houses, as viewed when looking upstream from Mitcham bridge in 1922.

Osier (willow) cutting for basket and hurdle making at the Watermeads at the turn of the century. The Watermeads were bought for the National Trust in 1913 and today are managed as a nature reserve.

The Wandle, flowing through 'Happy Valley', c.1930. This is part of the National Trust's Wandle properties.

The official opening of Ravensbury Park by George Lansbury (father of the actress, Angela Lansbury) on 10 May, 1930. Lansbury was, at the time, Commissioner of Works for the London County Council, which had contributed funds to save the area as a public park.

The Wandle flowing through Ravensbury Park, c.1930. The park was managed jointly by the borough of Mitcham and the urban district of Merton and Morden until their amalgamation in 1965 into the London Borough of Merton.

Cutting lavender at 3pm on July 20, 1904. Another of the photographs in the accurately documented series by the Croydon Camera Club. The main lavender industry had moved from Mitcham by the 1890s but a small number of growers continued into the twentieth century. The firm of Potter and Moore was established in Mitcham in the eighteenth century and the brand name has survived.

Outbuildings at The Willows, an eighteenth-century house in Willow Lane, which was pulled down in the 1920s. Louis Dutriez, a horticulturalist who ran a shop at Fair Green and occupied the premises in the 1890s, can be seen on the left with his granddaughter, Louise Martinne and grandson, Richard Martinne.

The opening of Hall & Co.'s cement-mixing plant in Willow Lane, *c.*1950. One of the first firms on the Willow Lane Estate, the company left its mark on the area in the form of gravel pits which were subsequently backfilled. The whole of the area has since been redeveloped as an industrial estate.

The unveiling of a plaque at Hengelo Gardens on the Ravensbury housing estate by the Burgomaster of Hengelo (Mitcham's twin town in Holland) on 30 August, 1952. Mr R. White, the Town Clerk, is on the left while Mr A. C. Prestage, the Mayor, is third from the right.

Seven

Education and Leisure

A photograph taken around 1925 of the former Upper Mitcham Boys' School, Commonside East which had been re-opened as Mitcham County School for Boys in 1922. It is now the St Thomas of Canterbury Middle School.

Boys from the Mitcham County School took all the parts in the annual Gilbert and Sullivan performances at the Baths Hall. On this occasion, 17 December, 1938, they are the guards and maidens in *Patience*. One of the major events of the Mitcham social calendar, the boys always played to packed houses.

Mayor Alderman D. Chalkely and the Mayoress congratulate the staff and boys of the Grammar School (the County School before the 1960s) on their success in the end-of-term music competition.

The Western Road School, opened in 1928 by Surrey County Council, the education authority for Mitcham, in 1954.

Class 2H of the Mitcham County School for Girls and their mistress, Miss Holbrook, in 1938. The building, which is next to the Wilson Hospital, is now occupied by the Cranmer Middle School.

Margaret Downing, May Queen of Gorringe Park Junior Mixed School, leads a procession of her attendants in 1936.

The infant school, part of the Lower Mitcham Schools (the Star Schools) in Benedict Road after a fire in 1901.

Lower Mitcham School for Girls, later the Benedict Junior School. This class photo dates from around 1920.

Sherwood Park Junior School, Abbotts Road, in 1950.

The swimming pool of the Alfred Mizen Primary School, Pollards Hill, in 1961. The Mizen family, market gardeners (see page 58), took a great interest in education and several members were prominent in local affairs.

Mitcham library which was built in 1933 on land donated by Joseph Owen (a local builder and one time Chairman of the Urban District Council) who also helped with the cost of the erection.

Some children show more interest than others in their books at Mitcham library in 1947.

An exhibition for children's book week in March 1947 in what was the reference library before the extension was built and is now used for storage. The group includes: Mr S.P.B. Mais; the Mayor (Alderman Mrs E. Watson); Councillor T.L. Ruff; the borough librarian (Mr D.H. Halliday); Alderman Cole and Mr Farrell (northeast divisional education officer).

Mitcham public library staff in July 1937. Left to right, standing: L.D. Gaze; W.E. Brown; H.C. Hallett; R.C. Hardy; C.F. Lovegrove; H.R. Jeffs; F. Walker; M.C. Norman. Seated: E. Cave; E.V. Corbett; K.G. Hunt (borough librarian); F.J. Gosling; C.R. Blake.

Pollards Hill library which was opened in 1970 and serves the Pollards Hill housing estate and surrounding area.

The opening of Colliers Wood library on 4 October, 1978.

The Mayor presents awards to exhibiting members of the Mitcham Camera Club in the 1950s.

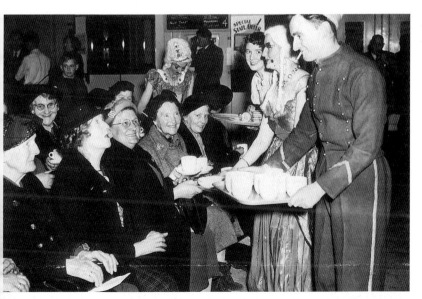

'Buttons' does the tea round during the interval of *Cinderella*, staged by Mitcham Works for the old folk of the district on 12 January, 1956.

A Mitcham Cricket Club group at the rear of the old Cricketers pub, c.1890. This building was bombed and replaced by the present building (see page 13).

The Mayor, J.P. Turner bowls the opening delivery of Mitcham cricket week in September 1937. Burn Bullock (see page 14) stands fourth from the left.

The beginning of a post-Second World War game between Mitcham and Surrey club and ground staff.

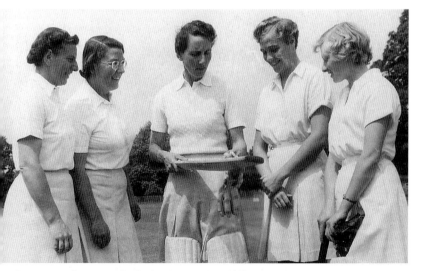

Surrey women's team on the Cricket Green in June 1958.

Lady members of the Mitcham bowling club at the back of the Canons in 1992.

A Southern Counties women's sports day in September 1954.

The Mitcham Comrades football team, 1921.

Tooting and Mitcham United Football Club playing Nottingham Forest at a packed Mitcham Stadium in January 1959.

Mitcham Korfball Team, 1962. Teams from Holland regularly visited Mitcham to play this game whose teams consisted of members of both sexes.

Swedish Athletes try their luck at the Mitcham Fête in August 1957.

Above: The Mayor (Alderman E.J.D. Field) hands the baton to the members of Mitcham Athletic Club at the start of the *News of the World* London to Brighton relay race in 1938 (see page 70).

Right: Ted Stepney with his cup for the best chrysanthemums at the Mitcham Show in 1938. The Stepney family ran a market garden business at the rear of Madeira Road for many years before moving out to Carshalton.

The Mitcham and District Lambretta club (the Goons), one of many scooter clubs in the '50s and '60s, in 1962.

Four competitors study the route card of the 1957 London Road Schools scouts rally. They are, from left to right: Alan Lovering, Ken Brookman, Dave Bradshaw and Alan Jones.

Eight

Public Service

Above: The Mitcham Town Guard, photographed around 1913. This auxiliary police force became part of the Special Constabulary in 1914.

Left: A 1924-view from the War Memorial across the south western corner of the Cricket Green showing the Almshouses in the distance. Between the War Memorial and the fenced clump of bushes is the site of the fire station. London Road runs across the picture and a tram standard is visible in the centre.

A newly-formed Home Guard unit outside Benningas, a margarine factory off Mortimer Road. One of many such units raised in 1940, this group had yet to be issued with their official uniforms. Members wore armbands on which LDV was printed, signifying they were Local Defence Volunteers.

An annual inspection of the Air Training Corps which began in the early 1940s to give boys some training before their call up. The organisation was heavily over-subscribed by youngsters with dreams of becoming fighter pilots and continues today. The aircraft recognition chart behind members of the 2157 squadron includes the Fairey Fulmar, the De Havilland Mosquito and a Gloucester Meteor, placing the photograph in the immediate post-war period.

The destruction caused by a High Explosive bomb dropped on Inglemere Road during the Blitz of 1940.

Bomb damage in Runnymede on 14 August 1940.

A crashed German Heinkel 111K twin-engined bomber displayed on the Cricket Green in aid of the local Spitfire fund, 2 October, 1940. An air raid warden (a member of the Civil Defence forces) studies the emblem which depicts the German eagle attacking the British lion.

The anti-aircraft emplacement on Mitcham Common, off Carshalton Road, to the south of Mitcham Junction station in 1961.

A public air raid shelter off Commonside East, near the Beehive Bridge, c.1955.

The 'Friar Tuck' British Restaurant in 1943. A very popular venue, especially with working people, the restaurant provided nutritious and reasonably-priced food to augment wartime rations.

A Remembrance Day parade passes the site of the bombed and yet to be rebuilt Cricketers pub in the centre and the Mitcham Town Hall on the right, 11 November 1951.

The Mayor, Councillor T.J. Higgs, visits the Home Guard graves at the London Road cemetery after a Remembrance Day service in 1957.

Left: Sir Isaac H. Wilson, local builder, benefactor and founder of the Wilson Hospital and the Mitcham Garden Village, providing homes for the elderly.

Opposite above: HRH Princess Mary inspects the guard of honour, provided by the local St John's Ambulance Brigade, under the command of Dr E. McIntyre, as part of the opening ceremony of the Wilson Hospital on 2 November, 1928.

Opposite below: The Wilson Hospital was supported by voluntary contributions and the annual fête was always well attended as here, on 14 June, 1957, despite the rainy conditions.

Below: The Wilson Cottage Hospital shortly before its opening in 1928.

The Victorian Mitcham police station which stood at the corner of Mitcham Park and the Cricket Green until its demolition in 1964 and replacement by the modern building.

Senior officers of the Metropolitan Police W Division, May 1945. Back row, from left to right: S.D. Insp. W.G. Jones; S.D. Insp. G.A. Siviour; S.D. Insp. C.S. Williams; S.D. Insp. A.C. Evans. Front row, D.D. Insp. J.R. Capstick; Chief Insp. H.J. Street; Sup. M.M. Miller; Chief Insp. J.A. Cole; Dist Insp. W.A. Ham.

Mitcham police and their collection of sports trophies in 1958.

'The Village Squirt' – Mitcham's venerable hand-operated, pony-drawn, fire pump which was regularly paraded in carnivals until the Second World War, when it was dismantled for scrap.

Opposite above: The private fire brigade of Pascall's sweet factory (see page 56) which was also available to the town in emergencies, in 1935.

Opposite below: A spectacular fire which began on 2 June, 1947 at the Willow Lane dump of tyres which had been collected for recycling during the war. The fire raged for days and a pall of black smoke could be seen from miles away.

Destruction to the houses on the east side of Belgrave Road caused by an explosion at the essential oils distillery of Messrs Bush & Co. on 30 March, 1933.

The explosion killed one small boy and caused the evacuation of many families for whom emergency provision was made.

Nine

Events, Celebrations
and Politics

The Maypole dance on Queen Victoria's Golden Jubilee, 1887, in front of the Lower Schools. The teachers who should have decorated the pole had gone to London to see the Queen and the children danced around a bare pole. Also visible are the rears of the Cricketers pub and the Vestry Hall.

Sports on Lower Green on Diamond Jubilee day, 1897. The late Victorian and Edwardian periods offered many opportunities for celebration – two jubilees and then two coronations. Mitcham was always ready to go en fête.

Charles Matthew's shop decorated for Edward VII's Coronation in 1901.

The 'Village Squirt' (see page 112), decorated for the Coronation of Edward VII crosses Upper Green. Killick's Lane (St Marks Road) is in the background.

A celebration at Hall Place, the home of Cato Worsfold, on the occasion of Canon Wilson's Jubilee in 1909. The bearded gentleman in the centre of the photograph is Canon Wilson who had been vicar of Mitcham since 1859. He is accompanied by his wife, who is holding a bouquet, and various members of Mitcham's 'nobility'.

An Elizabethan pageant on Lower Green, 22 June, 1911, part of the celebrations to mark the Coronation of George V.

The decorated float of the Camwal works, producers of aerated drinks, in a procession during the 1911 celebrations.

A street party, possibly in the Figges Marsh area, at the same time.

Above: A decorated float on Charter Day, 19 September, 1934, when the status of Mitcham was changed from an urban district (created in 1915) to that of a borough.

Left: The Charter Mayor, Robert Masters Chart and his wife and son, Stephen Chart, who became the first town clerk of Mitcham (photographed in 1934).

Right: A lavender seller, harking back to the heyday of Mitcham lavender production, is part of the Charter Day procession.

Below: The Potter & Moore float (see page 80) taking part in the Charter Day procession.

Sunday best for a party to mark the occasion of the Coronation of George VI in 1937.

The heavy decoration of this street in preparation for a party at the same time makes its identification very difficult!

A party after the Coronation of Elizabeth II in 1953 organised by the Bath Tavern on the Phipps Bridge Estate, near the houses affected by the explosion at Bush's (see page 114).

Queen Elizabeth, the Queen Mother, opening the Citizen's Advice Bureau in 1956.

A bonfire for Guy Fawkes night on Three King's Piece in 1958.

The Mayor crowns Mitcham's May Queen on the Cricket Green in May 1958, with the
Reverend John Thurrold and the Mace Bearer in attendance.

An orange and spoon race in Glebe Avenue keeps the children warm during the celebrations for
the Silver Jubilee of Elizabeth II in June 1977.

Mitcham Liberal Club in St Marks Road at the turn of the twentieth century.

The opening of 'Raydon', London Road, as the Conservative headquarters for the district, by Lord Middleton, c.1926.

A Mitcham and Wallington Labour Club social event at the Town Hall on 23 March, 1956.

A fancy-dress gathering on 2 February, 1939, outside the Lower Green parish room provides an opportunity for electioneering to Mr Cole, candidate in the following day's ward by-election. On the extreme left is Alderman A.H. Bailey whose wife is standing on the far right.

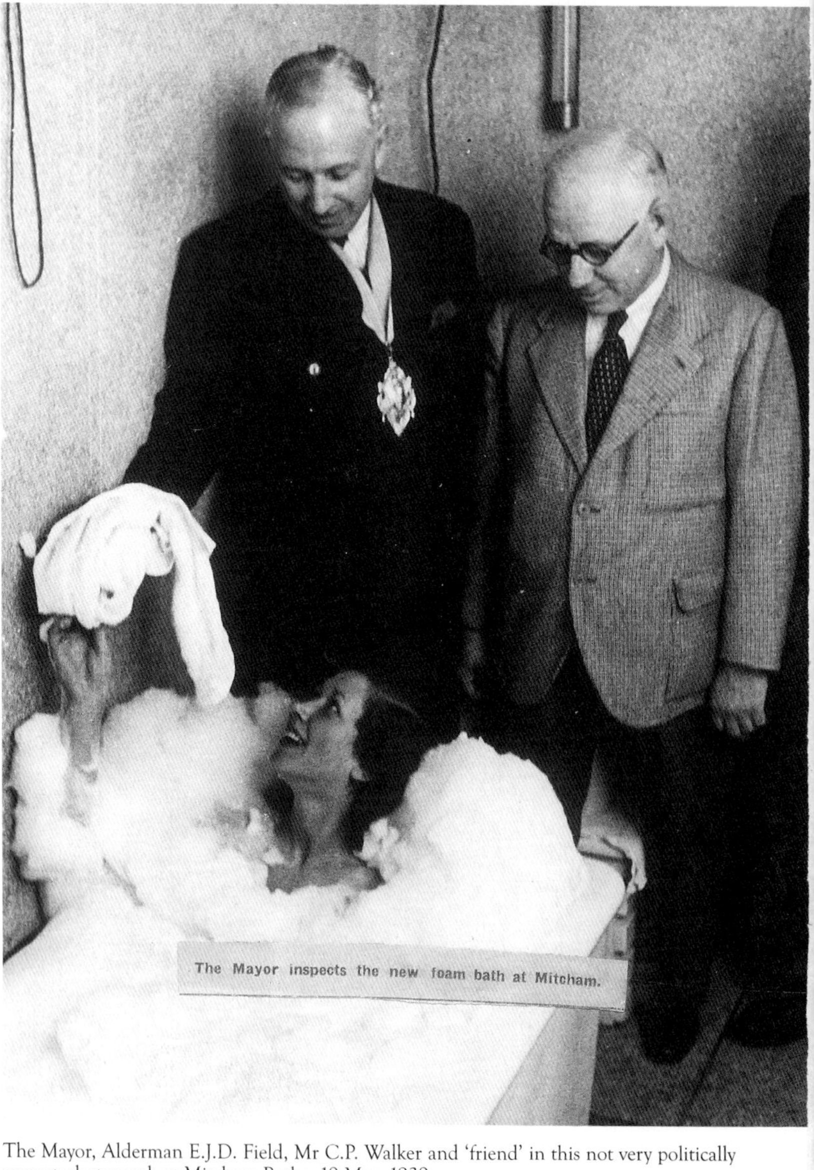
The Mayor inspects the new foam bath at Mitcham.

The Mayor, Alderman E.J.D. Field, Mr C.P. Walker and 'friend' in this not very politically correct photograph at Mitcham Baths, 19 May, 1939.